KAREN BROWN

Copyright © 2022 by Karen Brown

All rights reserved. Published in the United States by Title Your Truth Publishing, a division of Vision Publishing House, LLC.

Title Your Truth Publishing
hello@titleyourtruthpublishing.com
http://titleyourtruthpublishing.com

ISBN: 978-1-9552972-5-7 (Hardback)

No part of this book may be reproduced in any form or by any electronic or mechanical means, including information storage and retrieval systems, without written permission from the author, except for the use of brief quotations in a book review.

TABLE OF CONTENTS

Foreword 7
Preface 9
Acknowledgements 11

Decisions 15
Expose on Failures 18
Thought Chains 19
Expose on Love 22
Expose on Grief 24
One Way Out 27
#Selfie-Less 30
Expose on Guilt 31
Reject Me Not 32
Jealous-Sees 34
Expose on Mistakes 35
My Homeless Heart 37
Money Limits 40
To the Man-Kind 43
Nobody Knows 45
The Wrong Way 47
No, I'm Doing It! 48
Dear Believer 50
The Call 52
She Prayed For Me 54
Dear Me 56
Woman of Honor 58
Purposefully Living 59
Inside-Man Perspective 61
Expose on Anger 62

Addiction 63
Behind The Vow 65
Nothing To Give 67
Words Matter 69
Yes 70
They're Tellin' It 71
He Loves Us 73
Wanted 74
Expose on Lies 77
A God Conversation 80
Crucicidal 83
The Who-Nevers 85

About the Author 89

Foreword

This book is yet another example of how God will position one to have a tremendous impact on the lives of others. In her unyielding pursuit of God's purpose for her life, she has been led to write what I consider to be a book of critical instructions. My name is Jamaal Brown, and I am the oldest son of the author, Karen Brown. I have been given the honor of writing the foreword for this amazing book, which is very special, considering the fact that I am one of my mother's biggest critics.

The following story is intended to provide some insight into the life of the amazing woman responsible for this great literature:

It was May 30, 1995. Normally, my sister would be waking my brother and me up to get ready for school. Unfortunately, my brother and I were awakened by my sister's screams instead. She had just learned that our father, who had been battling cancer for many months in the room beneath us, had just passed on. He was a thirty-eight year-old loving father of four, with a fifth child on the way. I remember the image of my mother on the day of the funeral— pregnant, dressed in all black, walking down the seemingly endless two flights of steps at the front of our home in Baltimore, Maryland. The woman who had triumphed through many trials and tribulations– thanks to her strong faith in God– now had to deal with the loss of her mate of seventeen years, and the daunting task of becoming a single parent of five grieving children. And she did just that! I can speak for all my siblings when I say that we were so blessed to have such a wonderful mother.

Within Forbidden Conversations, my mother offers a wealth of wisdom and a lifetime of experience. Her love and compassion for people– if I may say so– is unmatched. In the book, she uses her God-given gift of poetry to enlighten us all regarding issues of the mind, body, and spirit. In "Words Matter," she speaks on the power of the tongue. I was blown away while reading "Exposé on Love" when she said true love is an irreversible decision. Wow! I had never thought of love that way before.

So prepare yourself to be enlightened, enriched, empowered, and inspired. My mother has invested her life into the service of caring for people. Through her writings, she has presented us all with an opportunity to experience an encounter with truth through her poetic gift.

                                          Enjoy and God Bless!

Preface

Forbidden Conversations is like a portrait I've painted throughout various seasons of my life. The pages of this book reveal themes that I have experienced in my own life or observed in the lives of others. I pray that these words incite positive inner and outer dialogues that will allow you to come face-to-face with your own forbidden conversations.

Acknowledgements

The completion of this book would not be possible without the love and support of many throughout my life. All of my experiences have shaped me into the woman I am today, forming the foundation for Forbidden Conversations to be birthed.

To my Lord, thank You so much for this journey. Throughout my life, there were moments when I felt helpless and defeated. Oftentimes, it seemed as if my failures laughed at me. Despite the challenges I experienced, You were always there for me. Without You, I would have lost my mind. It's a miracle that I'm still here.

To my loving husband, the late Ronald C. Brown, your legacy still continues and is revealed in the character and integrity of your children. Every now and then, I'll hear a phrase, observe a gesture, or catch a glimpse of an expression that reminds me that you are still here with us. Thank you for the life partnership we shared in raising four beautiful children, and for the fifth child you left in my womb. I know that if you were still here, you would be so proud of all of them. I honor your memory and give testimony to the great father and husband that you were. We'll always love you!

To my mom, the late Dorothy Hennigan, thank you for the opportunity to learn from your behavior and character. From watching you, I gained knowledge that was immensely valuable to me. Although such knowledge wasn't necessarily taught, it was caught! Mom, you were my poetry. My speech gives utterance to your "on-the-life" training. I never realized how many classes I took. You were my teacher for the woman I was to someday become. I watched you, taking subliminal notes for every test– revealing character, measuring patience, and developing integrity. It was through your struggles that I learned how to weather storms. And now, I speak to them with confidence, conviction, and certainty. I miss you and I'll always love you!

To my dad, Herman Lee, thank you for being the driving force of encouragement in this season in my life. You are a rock, even though your life has been hard. However, you remain steadfast and immovable. I love you, daddy. You are the source of my poetic flow. Keep writing, keep painting, and keep doing those pushups.

To all of my children– Kenia, Jamaal, Kaif, Imani, Imari, John, Tara, Tiffany, and Shirley (spiritual daughter)– thank you for all of your support and words of encouragement. Okay– maybe you didn't always encourage me, but your laughs and jokes made me more determined to get this work done!

To John and Kenia– thank you for promoting me on social media. Hey Kenia– #FirstbornYouAreMyMelody!

A special thank you to my son Jamaal and his beautiful wife, Mrs. Brownee– thank you for opening up your home and allowing me the time to work on several projects, including this book.

To my son Kaif and his new wife Tif– thank you for giving me the car that I really needed.

To mini me Imani a.k.a. baby girl, thank you for always being mommy's inspiration. You are truly #myface.

To my baby boy Imari– thank you for having my back! #IKnowYouLoveMe

To my grandchildren and great grandchildren, I love you all!

To my sister, Assata Nobles– thank you for all of your wisdom and for being a constant reminder that I'm only the oldest because I was born first. I love you!

To my Auntie Marilyn, thank you for loving and encouraging me.

To my niece Nef, thank you for being such a blessing to me.

To my nephew Nasia Lee, thank you for my beautiful cover design.

To my cousin Harriet, thank you for always being there for me.

To Apostle David Brown and Dr. Sharon Jackson, thank you for being instrumental in influencing my journey, as a woman of God.

To several very special ladies– the late Mother Mary Brown, Mother Rosa Lee Banks, and Mother Lisa Christian Green– thank you for graciously praying for me.

To Pastor Madeline Coxson, thank you for being there for me. You will always be my Mat Mat.

To Drena Bullock, thanks for opening up your home to me. It was a blessing.

To Muriel, thanks for welcoming me and my family into your space when we really needed it.

To my friend, Pastor Dana Neal, thank you for inspiring me to finish my book.

To my godchild KD, thank you for believing that someday I'll be famous.

Decisions

Now, someone you don't know
And everyone that you do
Has made a wrong choice-
Perhaps even you.

You're hurrying along,
Trying to keep up the pace,
You have to make this decision,
But you feel a delay.

And you try every angle
That you know to get through.
Could it be that your situation
Is speaking to you?

That yellow light in your life
Is a precautionary sign.
It means it's okay to proceed-
But wait- take your time.

Don't be too quick
Because you need to move slow.
And before you decide,
There's something else you should know.

Something is being hidden,
Slightly out of your view,
And it's none of my business,
But am I talking to you?

And then, there are times
When you're moving ahead
You know you can go,
But the light's clearly red.

Something inside
Telling you not to go
You're feeling the tension from within
And you know you should stop!

What you're doing!
It's not right; don't you see?
Your life is in danger!
Please, listen to me!

Don't be persuaded
Or tempted to go.
Did you hear what I said?
I said, "Tell them NO!"

Because it's not what you think
No, you will not escape.
They are not who they say they are.
This person is a fake.

But, I mind my own business,
And I don't have a clue.
I can't call no names,
But am I talking to you?

So wait for that situation
In your life to turn green.
It's when your heart and your mind
And your spirit agree.

When the anxiousness has ceased,
And your vision is clear
And the voice that really loves you,
Is the voice that you hear.

Saying, "Don't go down that road
Unless you're absolutely sure…
Because some mistakes cost a little,
But others cost a lot more."

And don't try to save face;
It's the worst thing you can do.
I'm minding my own business,
But I think I'm talking to you.

Expose On Failures

Failures are like uninvited guests
Who come into your home
And keep making excuses
For not wanting to leave.
>They walk around in your life
>Constantly wanting to be entertained.
>>They sit around all day
>>Watching old videos
>>And laughing at how well
>>They performed in your life.

Their perception of the future
Is a repeat of the past.
>As soon as you start
>Talking about trying again,
>They throw you a surprise —
>Been-there-done-that party!
>>They invite celebrities like
>>Someday I'll, Procrastination, Fear,
>>And that's just to name a few.

By the time they finish with you,
You will have smoked doubt,
Inhaled fear,
Drank unbelief,
And be left
Hung over
Your failures
Forever.

Thought Chains

I'm locked in here
And I can't get out.
My thoughts are the guards
And I hear them about,

Making the plans
For my quick demise.
They keep telling me stories
And telling me lies.

Every day, they tell me
That I don't measure up.
They say, "Look in the mirror,
You're really a nut.

And who do you think
Is going to listen to you?
Stop living your dream.
It's over. You're through.

You have nothing to offer
And nobody cares.
Just look all around you.
There's nobody there."

I don't understand why
I'm acting so strange.
I drink; I take drugs.
I know it's time for a change.

But how do I get past
These thoughts in my mind?
I'm crying for help.
I hope someone can find

Me in time
Before life passes away,
And I lose my tomorrows
For the mistakes of today.

Then, a miracle happens
Unexpectedly
When I hear a voice
Deep inside of me.

"It's time to change the guards,"
That's what the voice said.
"Your thoughts are the problem.
Get them out of your head."

So, I approached those thoughts
That were swirling around in my head.
I did not let them hear me,
As I listened to the words that were being said

"You can't do this,
And you can't do that.
You're stupid. You're lazy.
Too skinny! Too fat!"

"But I'm really going to make it
'Cause I've made up my mind."
"Oh, give me a break.
You said that the last time.

And you obviously
Don't have a clue
That the thoughts in your head
Are the thoughts that you'll do.

You're full of ideas
That other people get done,
But how many have you completed?
Absolutely, none!"

Well, I couldn't believe my ears
And the words that were being said.
This was dialogue for destruction
Taking place up in my head.

I got so mad and angry
As I realized the years that I spent.
My negative thoughts were defeating me
And my dreams– that were God sent.

So, I went right to my mind
And told those thoughts they had to go.
And the only reason they stayed this long
Was because I didn't know.

Expose On Love

Who has known love?
One thing is true.
If you've ever truly loved anyone,
It is impossible to ever stop loving them.

For it is on the grounds that
Most people abandon love,
That true love
Chooses to remain.

It has been stated that
Love is an emotion,
But true love
Is an irreversible decision.

True love can
Express emotion,
But it cannot
Be defined by it.

Emotions are feelings
That are subject to change.
Therefore,
They cannot be trusted.

True love, however,
Is constant,
Unwavering,
And steadfast in its dedication.

It is unconditional
From beginning to end.
It doesn't seek anything,
Nor does it expect anything
In return for its dedication.

True love uses forgiveness
To cover an offense.
It uses patience to cover agitation,
Kindness to cover hostility.

True love can be firm,
But not harsh.
It can convict,
But it does not condemn.

It builds up,
But it does not tear down.
So then,
Who has known love?

EXPOSE ON GRIEF

Who can describe the pain that comes
When your loved one goes away?
In the distance, you see the smiles
And you hear the kind words people say.

But don't they know,
And can't they see
That the person they think they're talking to
Really isn't me?

For I've gone away for a while.
Grief came to get me last night.
And she promised to bring me back someday.
When I asked her "How soon?"
She wouldn't say.

She took me to a dark, lonely place
Somewhere inside of me
To replace the life I have
In exchange for memories,

Where I cry a lot
And my tears just flow.
I've tried to go back to myself,
But grief won't let me go.
She says, "You need more time,"
And when I'm ready, she'll let me know.

Some friends came to visit
Just the other day.
Grief told them I was doing fine,
Then, she sent them all away.

As she closed the door behind them,
She posted up a sign,
"Please do not disturb.
I am away from my mind."

Grief sits with me and talks with me a lot,
Mostly about the past.
She seems to enjoy my tears,
But she frowns whenever I laugh.

She sings the same sad songs
About my loved one who went away.
I found myself consoling her.
Then, I knew this was the day.

I could return to myself
To live out the rest of me
For it became obvious
That grief had no intention of
Ever setting me free.

So, I packed up all my sadness,
And I put away my pain.
I put my loved one's memories
In a box that had their name.

I wrapped it very nicely,
So it would not come apart.
Now, the life we shared together
Is forever in my heart.

                "I'll always love you." [whisper]

Then, I told grief I was leaving,
And I handed her my key.
Her voice tone changed to anger.
In disgust, she looked at me.

"I brought you in my home
And I gave you comfort every day.
I've been there every moment
Since your loved one went away.

I brought you all those pictures
And I sang you all those songs.
I let you cry for hours
While I watched you sadly mourn.

Where on earth could you ever find
That kind of loyalty?
And you pay me back like this?"
Those were the words she said to me.

Then, I closed the door behind me
To bring my grieving to an end.
Yes, grief did give me comfort,

            But she never ever was my friend. [whisper]

One Way Out

Run... run...
As fast as you can!
Run from your guilt
Or take a stand.

                Where will you go
             And what will you do?
          To escape that bad feeling
                That comes over you?

It's the memory of
That wrong that was done
That triggers the guilt
From which you cannot run.

           You thought that with time
              It would all go away,
         But it's more real right now
             Than it was yesterday.

And who can you tell
To get some relief
From the burdensome weights
Of your lies and deceit?

                                        Run... run...
                                    As fast as you can!
                                      Run from your guilt
                                            Or take a stand.

The truth being told
Was your biggest fear,
But the torment of guilt
Is much more to bear.

                            And the fact that you won't
                                  Admit to your wrong,
                      Gives guilt rights to move in
                            And build a strong– hold

Right in your mind
To make sure you get caught.
So now, you're a fugitive
Running from your own thoughts.

And who ever heard
Of doing time in your head?
No peace; you can't sleep–
And you wish you were dead!

                        Run... run...
                      As fast as you can!
                      Run from your guilt
                          Or take a stand.

Stop living in hell;
Go face what you've done.
That hurt that you've caused
Was done to someone.

                      Go to that person
                      And ask to be forgiven,
                    They may have passed on,
              Or perhaps they're still living.

Then forgive yourself
And tell guilt it can't stay.
Set yourself free,
And then walk away.

#SELFIE-LESS

No doubt, these are perilous times that we live in.
Unfortunate circumstances can knock on our door at any time.
It's so easy to pass judgment on others,
While sitting back and marveling at
How good the hand, that life has dealt our way

Who can count the tears cried
During a despairing season in someone's life?
If only we would have been more attentive,
We would have seen the tears forming behind the eyes
Of someone less fortunate than ourselves

Had we not have been so busy consuming ourselves with ourselves,
We would have heard their desperate cries of despair.
Perhaps in some small way, a burden could have been lifted
By an extended hand that reached out to help.

Perhaps, that extended hand could have been my own.

Exposé on Guilt

EACH OF US CAN IDENTIFY WITH THE DARK FEELING
THAT COMES FROM HAVING DONE SOMETHING WRONG.
IF A PROOF IS THE EVIDENCE THAT A PICTURE HAS BEEN TAKEN,
THEN GUILT IS THE EVIDENCE THAT A WRONG HAS BEEN COMMITTED.
SOMETIMES THE WRONG IS REAL, BUT OFTENTIMES IT'S IMAGINED.

IN ANY CASE, GUILT IS RESPONSIBLE FOR LEAVING ITS VICTIMS
SCRAMBLING FOR DRUGS, ALCOHOL, AND SOMETIMES EVEN DEATH, ITSELF.
IN A RECENT INTERVIEW, GUILT WAS ASKED TO RESPOND TO THESE ALLEGATIONS
AND GAVE THE FOLLOWING RESPONSE:

"I'VE BEEN FALSELY ACCUSED AND TOTALLY MISUNDERSTOOD.
MANKIND THINKS OF ME AS AN ENEMY, WHEN IN REALITY,
I'M THE DARK CLOUD THAT COMES INTO A PERSON'S LIFE
TO TORMENT THEM FOR SOME REAL OR IMAGINED WRONG THAT THEY'VE DONE.
I USUALLY SHOW UP WHEN THE PERSON WHO HAS COMMITTED THE WRONG
IS PLANNING TO CONCEAL IT OR REFUSE TO ACKNOWLEDGE IT.

NOW, I ADMIT THAT THERE ARE TIMES WHEN I TAKE ADVANTAGE OF INNOCENT PEOPLE,
WHO ALREADY FEEL BAD; I JUST MAKE THEM FEEL WORSE.
BUT, BEFORE YOU JUDGE ME, LET ME GO ON RECORD
HAVING MADE THIS FINAL STATEMENT.

MY NAME IS GUILT AND I'M THE DARK CLOUD THAT HANGS OVER A PERSON'S LIFE
FOR HAVING DONE SOMETHING WRONG— REAL OR IMAGINED
THAT THEY ARE PLANNING TO CONCEAL OR REFUSE TO ACKNOWLEDGE.
I MAKE NO APOLOGIES FOR IT BECAUSE THAT'S WHAT I WAS CREATED TO DO.
MY BIGGEST FEAR IS THE TRUTH THAT JESUS CHRIST CAME TO SET THEM FREE,
AND WHEREVER THAT TRUTH IS REALIZED, YOU WILL NEVER FIND ME!"

Reject Me Not

How do I move past rejection?
That feeling of not being wanted–
Ever!

Never being chosen
As a child to play.
"Stay here,"
They say.

"We don't want you."

Few people understand life,
Being different and not fitting in.
When they see you, but look past—
Fast forwarding their glance

To someone—
Who looks like,
Sounds like,
And dresses like the crowd.

How difficult it is to be comfortable
In your own skin—
To discipline
Your heart to love 'self.

Healthy thoughts are the key.
You must relentlessly
Cherish your difference
That makes you great!

Why wait for them to embrace you?
You must embrace yourself, first
'Cause self-hate is a curse.

Remember to put on confidence.
It's the magnet that attracts
And makes people wonder
How you can

Love you,
Flaunt you,
And be determined to be you–
No matter who you are or what you look like.

Jealous-Sees

Jealous-sees **HATE** —
Extreme hostility disguised through a grin
Cold glances
Evil trances
Mean stares
Victims, beware!

Jealous-sees **ENVY** —
Those covetous desires
Like raging fires blistering from within
Secretly they wait,
Determined at any cost to do you in.

Jealous-sees **ENMITY** —
A war between opposing views and ideas,
Conflicting conflicts
Diabolical schemes
Hidden plans for your demise
Enemies forever
And you don't know why.

Jealous-sees **YOU** —
An unsuspecting victim caught in a web of deceit
By someone who is overtly impressed.
They want your dreams and your talent;
With your life, they are obsessed.

VICTIMS BEWARE!

Expose' On Mistakes

I've never met a soul so stricken with grief,
And I've never heard a cry like the cry for relief.

From a moment in time when something took place,
It was a mistake in the past that couldn't be erased.

Each moment we meet from the time that we met,
To discuss that mistake as if I could forget.

I can't count the times rehearsed in my head,
From the time I get up 'til I go back to bed.

The mistake that I made is much bigger than me.
It's a constant reminder that I'll never be free.

The weight of the guilt that I carry each day
Is the price for the peace that I lost along the way.

Each moment we meet from the time that we met
To discuss that mistake that I really regret.

A mistake that should live in the back of my mind
Is making demands and it's stealing my time.

That mistake cost me yesterday; it threatens tomorrow.
My future's uncertain, while I bathe in my sorrows.

Haven't you ever made a mistake; do you carry it around?
And are you bearing the weight of something in life?

That you simply can't change?
It keeps taunting you, Stalking you–
Calling your name.

Listen!

It's not in your power to go back to that day
To relive that moment; you can't take it away.

There are no erasers– no whiteout, no tape.
There's no magic formula to help you erase.

Because mistakes are just common, not exclusive to you.
Ask anyone in life because they've made mistakes, too.

So stop all this madness of day in and out pain.
You're not going crazy; so tell yourself that you're sane.

Go look in the mirror and tell the person you see
That the person who made that mistake is not me!

I'm sorry for decisions that I made in the past.
I feel guilty 'cause I messed up, but how long should the guilt last?

I can't live like this; I have to let go.
I'm taking my life back– no more feeling low!

No more saying sorry because I've done that a lot.
I've been too hard on myself. And excuse me– but I'm not

Going to live life like this anymore.
God has something better, so I'm closing this door.

So now when I go to the mirror and I look at the image of me,
I pray, Lord forgive me for all my mistakes and complete your work in me.

Homeless Heart

Looking back through passing visions,
I see myself as a child shattered—
Emotionally battered by my own surroundings.
Weeping, tears streaming, pleading for those
traumatic tsunamis to cease.
Saying words, but not being heard.
Yelling and screaming at my heart
To respond to the pain it could no longer feel.
Trying to heal, but as time passed time,
I became separated from my heart—
The love in my life.

Logging into my life, I search for me
On the net of my emotions, lacking devotions,
Too much commotion— no strings.
Detachment is necessary.
My heart is growing weary of days ahead,
No place to lay my head and rest from -
The secrets in my life.

Trapped in an avalanche of emotion,
Inner turmoil is always approaching.
I feel myself riding high,
Trying to escape my lows.
Reality gets mixed in with confusion,
And my fantasy is the illusion.
If I could only take a moment to breathe
Without the air, that suffocating air—
Those pressures in my life

Standing on the banks of a river within
The undercurrent of pain drifting
Dreams shifting from place to place
In my own shadow I stand
To try to listen to my own heartbeat
Because that's where the real me lies
I feel tears that I can't cry.
And I hear words that I can't speak.
Seeking answers without having
Asked the right questions,
And my heart keeps asking me–
About the pain in my life?"

Glancing ahead, I hear my destiny
Calling me to a place where I can face
My failures, my faults, and my fears.
I see me saying "no," refusing to let
My negative past go with me—
telling it to stop! Excuse me!
But you're not the beginning
and the end of me-
The walkways in my life.

Then, I see me in my future,
Impressively dressed
Dangling the keys to new doors,
and my desires leading me to more—
Of the unlimited possibilities in my life.

MONEY LIMITS

The best things in life
Are things money can't buy.

It can't buy you peace
In a moment of stress.
It can't buy you sleep
When your body can't rest.

It can't buy a friend
Because no price can be paid.
True friends are not brought,
With time they are made.

                    Money can't buy joy,
              That feeling from within
              That's so overwhelming
                    You can't keep it in.

                        It can't buy words
            That come from the heart,
          Expressing the gratitude
                Of being a part.

                    And sharing life
            With someone you love,
                  That is a gift
           And it comes from above.

MONEY CAN'T BUY
THE SILENT PLEAS–
WARNINGS OF DANGERS
THAT WE COULD NOT SEE.

THEY CAME FROM OUR LOVED ONES
SO LONG AGO.
IF ONLY WE'D LISTENED BACK THEN,
WE WOULD KNOW

THAT THEY WEREN'T REALLY TRYING
TO STIFLE OUR FUN.
THEY DID THOSE SAME THINGS
BACK WHEN THEY WERE YOUNG,

THEY TOO WERE DECEIVED,
AND THEY PAID A PRICE.
SO, THEY WARNED US TO KEEP IT
FROM HAPPENING, TWICE.

MONEY CAN'T BUY THE TIME SHARED
WITH FAMILY AND FRIENDS
PRECIOUS MOMENTS IN LIFE
THAT SOMEDAY WILL ALL END

AND SOME OF THOSE MOMENTS
WE WISH WE HAD NOT SHARED.
WE HURT THOSE WE LOVED
WHEN OUR TEMPERS WERE FLARED.

OH, THEY HURT US, TOO,
BUT WE COULD NOT SEE
THAT THE PASSING OF TIME
FADES ALL MEMORIES.

SO THERE, THEY STAY FROZEN
SOMEWHERE IN THE PAST–
THE JOYS, THE TEARS,
THE SORROWS, THE LAUGHS

MONEY CAN'T BUY
THAT BACK AND NOBODY KNOWS,
WHEN THEIR LIFE ON THIS EARTH
WILL COME TO A CLOSE.

You can never really repay
Your last respects to the dead,
Because the last time you saw them,
You already did.

TO THE MAN-KIND

BROTHERS,

BETTER STOP CHASING DREAMS
THAT TURN INTO NIGHTMARES.
BETTER STOP BEING A SUCKER FOR
A NICE BODY, PRETTY FACE
FLAT WAIST, BUT HER MIND IS LACED
WITH A SUBCONSCIOUS OF BEAUTY OVER MATTER.

BETTER STOP BEING WOOED BY
MAC, MAYBELLINE, AND CHANEL
THAT MAKES THEM LOOK GREAT!

GET PAST YOUR HASTE TO LAY THEM DOWN
INSTEAD OF TURNING UP THE VOLUME OF THEIR VOICES
TO SEE WHAT'S IN THEIR HEAD
THAT GOES BEYOND THE BED.

BETTER STOP BEING DECEIVED BY THE WEAVE
THAT— IT'S OKAY TO WEAR,
BUT WHEN SHE TAKES IT OFF,
IS THERE ANYTHING THERE?

BETTER STOP PLAYING YOURSELF WITH TIME WASTED
TRYING TO BE THE MAN
GOING IN AND OUT LIKE AN ETERNAL FOUNTAIN
THINKING YOU STILL HAD IT LIKE THAT AND YOU USED TO.

BETTER GO FIND THE ONE WHO'S A KEEPER
WHO'S GOT YOUR BACK.
LET HER BE THE ONE TO MOTHER YOUR CHILDREN,
CULTIVATE YOUR DREAMS,
AND BELIEVE IN YOUR VISION.
UNDERSTAND THAT HER PRICE IS FAR ABOVE RUBIES
AND NO WOMAN THAT YOU DESIRE CAN COMPARE WITH HER.

Sincerely Yours,

Wisdom

NOBODY KNOWS

Nobody knows that my smile is a lie, sometimes.
It is part of a conspiracy to cover up tangled emotions,
Pain, scars, and inside tears that have no way out,
Because my smile is a lie that won't let me be true.

My smile is the lie that got me to this place.
You see, nobody really enjoys a sorrowful face.
It reflects the truth that there's pain somewhere
And God forbid, if we would have to care
About someone else's pain that's not our own.
So I smile this lie to keep me from
Expressing what's really inside

A lying smile emerged when my
Friends betrayed my trust
And nobody knows the wounds that come
From someone you let get close,

    It hurts the most.
      I was hemorrhaging from within
          Hyperventilating to grin past my pain
            To smile again

And nobody knows the trouble that I carry
I've died from careless words spoken.
People were laughing and joking
At my pain, but I did not let them know.

    I did not let it show
        But my masquerading smile
            Was concealing a hurt that was so deep.
          I wish I could weep,
            I wish I could cry,
              And cry
                And cry

And expose this lie
That my smile wears.

Strip down and let you see me bear
My frustrations and heartaches
And tell you
All my secret woes
That nobody knows

And the pain that people have
inflicted on me.
It goes so deep
That I can't let you see me weep...

I weep alone!

THE WRONG WAY

YOU FEEL LIKE YOU'RE LOST,
TAKING ALL THE WRONG TURNS.
YOU KEEP MAKING BAD CHOICES.
STOP!

WHEN WILL YOU LEARN
THAT IT DOESN'T REALLY MATTER
WHAT OTHER PEOPLE SAY?
IT'S WHEN YOU CAN ADMIT TO YOURSELF,
"SELF, I'M GOING THE WRONG WAY!"

No, I'm Not Doing It!

Using your own mind,
Creating your own thoughts
To make your own choices
But can you ignore the voices

Speaking into your ear
Trying to get you
To do what they say,
But can you just walk away

From your peers that laugh at you
And stare when you say you won't go
But can you really tell them "NO,"

And mean it when you say
Stop! Excuse me!
But I'm not like everyone else
Because I can be by myself.

When everyone else is doing it
But I'm not really feeling it
And I say "No!
I'm not doing it."

Because I'm using my own mind,
Creating my own thoughts,
And making my own choices

I can ignore the voices.
trying to convince me to
Leave myself to become
Something that I'm not

So, I tell myself to stop
And I choose to do me.

Dear Believer

I live life on the dark side
Where wickedness reigns and evil resides.
Sinner is my name
And sinning is the game.
I play to win
Other opportunities to sin.

When I lay down at night
And reflect on my sins,
I feel guilt that's so heavy.
It's like a prison that I'm in.
There are things that I've done,
Much too shameful to express!
But what's more fearful than that
Is what I might do next!

So, I'm crying for help because I want to be free,
But is there one Believer who'll share the Gospel with me?

It's amazing to watch Believers passing us by
Lord knows in my heart, I just want to ask them why?
Or how did they forget their life before the Cross?
Did I miss something? 'Cause in the Word, wasn't everybody lost?
And the truth of this new life that you're privileged to embrace,
Is that now when you sin, you're under a new law called grace.
And I need that new law working in my life.
Last I heard it was still free; now y'all know that ain't right!

So, I'm crying for help 'cause I want to be free,
But is there one Believer who'll share the Gospel with me?

You see, time's passing by and our numbers are growing,
Sinners are dying; some not really knowing
That the fruit of their labor is a fiery hell—
One they could have avoided, had they been compelled
To listen to a message about a bloodstained Cross,
And a Savior who was crucified to keep them from being lost.

Yeah, I'm crying for help because I want to be free,
But not just for myself, but for others like me.

Sincerely,

A Sinner

The Call

A person doesn't sleep at night,
Because that's when the clouds roll in.
Monologues and dialogues of thoughts—

Where have you been?
And what have you done
To cause your sleep to run?

Too many secrets hidden from the day,
But then comes the night.
And it's time to play back
Secrets in the past;
Times and events
That use your nighttime to vent.

Where did you go?
And what did you see
To cause your sleep to hide?

Oh, sleepy one,
Only you know why.
You hear the cries,
And you know the lies,
That promised to keep
You safe from the truth.

Sometimes, you have
To go back and do things right.
Revisit the nights in your life.
Your past wants an opportunity to meet.

You can't go through life making a mess
If you expect to find true happiness.
And if your future has
Any hope at all
Then your past
must be given

A call.

She Prayed For Me

Did you know her?
Love flowing through her like a river-
So gentle
So sweet
So kind

I never heard her complain,
But I could see her pain
Behind that smile.

Hiding her sorrows
And her woes
Her tears held back
And did you know?

She prayed for me
When I would call
To pray for her,
She would pray for me.

Did you see her
In the marketplace?
Did she light up your face?
You, too! She had this grace.

And it didn't matter who you were
Or where you were in your life.
She had a way of making your day bright.

Did you listen to her?
Trying to give you some wisdom from a deep place
Some sorrows, some trials,
And perhaps some mistakes

Her voice when she spoke
Seemed to echo warnings from her past,
Did she touch you
Gently- with a hug or an embrace?

Did it make you feel
Some kind of way
Like love
Touching you?

Did you try to run away from her love?
God's love in her reaching out
To all she would meet
God bless you, Mother

Rest in Peace

Dear Me

I've been wanting to talk to you about your life.
You seem so preoccupied with everyday situations
That you haven't taken the time to really get to know me.
I watch you get up every day,
Go to the mirror, look at yourself and walk away
Not realizing who you are.
You spend so much time focusing on the outer you,
That you totally neglect me, your inner man.
Although we're the same person,
I see things from a different perspective.
Your flesh (outer man) craves immediate gratification
Without regard for long term consequences.
As your inner man, I use wisdom and prudence as a guide.
I see beyond the surface into the spirit.
Whenever you get an uneasy feeling about something or someone,
That's my way of warning you that something is just not right.
There have been times when opportunities came your way
And you were so excited!
That was me jumping up and down on the inside of you
Like a cheerleader encouraging you to go ahead.
But you ignored my voice and listened to those inner lies,
Telling you that the possible was impossible.
Your philosophy on life is this,
If it looks and feels good, then it's okay to do it.

But you've never stopped to consider the outcome.
Until now, you're the one who's been making
Most of the decisions with regard to our life.
I wanted to write you to tell you
Not to forget me; I'm in here too!
I don't expect you to consult me on every decision.
But on matters that are not obvious to the human mind,
You need my input.
Start paying more attention to your dreams
And those unexplainable emotions that seem
To come out of nowhere.
Use peace and joy as a green light to
Determine what you should do.
Let bad feelings, fear, and anxiety
Be your yellow and red lights in life.
Remember that we are a team
Striving to achieve our purpose and fulfill our destiny.

Sincerely,

You

WOMAN OF HONOR

What honor should the woman receive,
Who brings forth a child and then soon she leaves?
Forsaking the love that she felt deep inside,
Knowing someday the child will ask, "Why?"

"Why did you leave me alone in this world?"
Your precious son or your baby girl
The answer to that question still haunts her today.
Too many voices led her down the wrong way.

She tried and she tried to get back to her life.
She still carries the guilt for not making things right.
But her honor should come from the choice that she made
To give the child life when she didn't see a way.

Purposefully Living

Who am I and for what purpose was I created?

If I accomplish everything that I set out to do in life,
But neglect the purpose for which I was created.
Who will give an account for me?

When I come to life's end,
Will my achievements give an account for my life?
Will they become witnesses in my defense
For not fulfilling my purpose?

What if I receive the awes of men
For living a life of grandeur
That made me the envy of all?

Will the awes of men be given an
Opportunity to testify on my behalf
For not having fulfilled my purpose?

What if I lead the masses to the
Fulfillment of their dreams?

Can their dreams become a documentary
To be used in my defense for not
Having fulfilled my purpose?
Certainly not!

For to receive the awes of men
For my notable achievements is honorable.

To have acquired fame
For living a life of wealth and grandeur
That made me the envy of all is admirable.

To lead others to the fulfillment
Of their dreams is commendable,

But to muffle the voice of purpose
Within makes life miserable.

When my life comes to an end
My purpose will take the stand
And eloquently declare
That in light of all that was achieved,

Failure to fulfill purpose
Is a life lived aimlessly.
So then, where is purpose,
And who can find it?

**Purpose is found in the mind of the Creator,
And it is found by those who diligently seek Him!**

Inside Man Perspective

I'm standing here inside myself and looking all around.
There's inventory everywhere- so high, it's falling down.
My gifts are stacked so neatly, and my talents are all in rows
But when asked the value of them all, I really didn't know.

The skills I'd worked so hard to get were beautifully displayed,
And whenever I'd share my inventory, people were so amazed.
"You're really great," they'd tell me, and "Your talents are quite rare.
You've got something so special," but I replied with just a stare.

I'd never seen myself from inside out of me before.
I'd never taken inventory of this hidden store.
I'd spent my years discovering the things my eyes could see,
but my truer self is now unveiled- this hidden mystery.

I've felt the shutters of success, ignored their constant pleas
To go beyond complacency to be all that I could be!
I made those resolutions for the year when it came in.
I'd sadly taste my failures when the year came to an end.

I'm standing here inside myself, taking inventory of me
The gains, the losses, the price- the cost of facing reality
You see, I failed to ignore the voices that would speak inside my head.
There was doubt, fear, and unbelief- by their counsel I was led.

The truth behind the voices, those wandering thoughts with vicious intent
They came to rob me of my purpose, and my destiny that was God sent.
I'm standing here inside myself with inventory, everywhere.
In desperation I cry out, but nobody seems to care.

You see, I know there's greatness in me, and how
I long to get it out. Another day goes, but
Tomorrow knows that it doesn't have to be the same
Because getting the inside out and the
Outside in, is a guarantee for change.

EXPOSE' ON ANGER

The boiling emotion is the way to describe
The state of a man's soul where anger abides.

Oh, anger, how your temper flared with non-controlling rage!
What caused your spirit to erupt beyond your human gauge?

You heard, you saw, you felt, and then,
You stepped outside of the soul you were in
And no one saw it take control,
But an evil wind swept
Through your soul.

Then, we saw fiery eyes of fury,
And we heard your heart beat hate,
Your soul cried out for mercy,
But the cry came much too late!

Oh, anger, how your temper flared with uncontrollable rage!
What caused your spirit to erupt beyond your human gauge?

Addiction

My addiction came to me
Dressed in persuasion, hiding
Discreetly behind my fears.

I see you there dangling my chains like bling bling,
Trying to convince me to be weak again and just give in.

Like a pimp, my addiction knows the power
Of control over me and my senses.
And one by one, I watched them being seduced.

My eyes gave up their vision
For illusionary projections of my addiction doing me.
We'd been here before and those mental images of my first time
With my addiction and the bliss we shared.

And even then, I was scared
Because I knew that I'd never be
Able to forget that taste in my mouth–
Not for life, but for more of my addiction.

I felt my tongue dancing, seductively,
Sending messages like emails to the rest of me,
Trying to get a response immediately,
And although I knew it was wrong,
It wasn't long before I smelt that scent.

Those fumes of love being worn
Like perfumed-cologne by my addiction.
Then I really started tripping, my heart started skipping
And it was too late because I knew I'd been played.

There I was, standing in an aromatized state
About to give in, and I didn't want to win.
Because I was waiting for the touch from my addiction
Erogenously zoning me, owning me everywhere–
And I didn't care.

Those tingling sensations conspiring against me
And my body was on fire with more desire for my addiction.
My addiction watched me beg and plead
Punishing me for trying to leave.

And as I stood outside of myself
Horrified by my willingness to surrender my dignity
For lying pleasures and losing illusions.

Then I heard my voice speak
In desperation and ask the question:
"How do I escape that which I hate, but love to experience?"
That high that keeps taking me low to the gutter of my soul
In and out of a battle that I win,
But lose each time I do it again.

And get up only to go down
Pleading for my life, saying "Noooo and yes!"
This time, things will be different from the past.
And my future is the dream
That wakes me up from my addiction.

BEHIND THE VOW

Beyond the bliss, beyond the kiss
Of preconceived devotion,
The marriage vow, a debt of love
Is more than just a notion.

This sparkling day, it glitters like gold,
But the secrets thereof are yet to unfold.
As bride and groom proceed to wed
And to consummate their love in the wedding bed.

But the bed whispers softly,
"This love that you feel now is temporary at best.
True love will come after you've gone through some tests."

Then, the sheets make their plea.
"The warmth in your eyes may someday turn cold
From the heartbreaks you'll give to each other;
Argumentative displays and heated arrays,
As your true selves are revealed to each other."

Then, the pillow starts to talk, and it says
"Your heart doesn't know and your mind can't conceive
What this vow that you've made will require.
Not knowing your fate
And what you don't know about your mate,
Make this life that you chose less desired."

So, prepare for the laughter, the joys, and the bliss,
But while you're preparing, prepare also for this.

Prepare for the moments of silent despair.
Prepare for the loneliness, even when someone's there.

Prepare for the times when you will not be heard,
When more precious than gold are your unspoken words.

Prepare for some fun times- those high mountain top times.
Prepare for those "oooh" times- those loving my boo times.

Prepare to have hope when things look dim and bleak.
Prepare to be strong when your partner is weak.

Prepare to forgive and not to carry the weights
Of the faults and mistakes of an imperfect mate.

Because that load gets too heavy, and the grief's hard to bear.
True love soon grows cold, 'till one day nothing's there.

Prepare to be patient. It's a virtue you must acquire,
'Cause no price can be paid for love that's been tested in the fire.

Prepare to wake up to the person you thought you knew,
And in your mind, ask the question, "Who in hell are you?"

Prepare to give a lot and to receive very little in return,
Because life isn't always fair. Embrace that truth and you will learn

To look past imperfection- to the person that's within,
To overlook their failures, and put your focus on their wins.

And finally, learn to speak encouraging words.
Affirmations are the seeds of love
That find their way into the human heart
And give birth to more love and to making love more.

NOTHING TO GIVE

I THOUGHT I HAD NOTHING TO GIVE,
AND SO, I SAID TO MYSELF,
"I WILL GIVE MY SILENCE AWAY AS A GIFT."

TO LISTEN AND NOT SAY ANYTHING,
WHILE SURGES OF EMOTIONS, OPINIONS, AND ADVICE
THAT I KNEW WAS RIGHT.

BUT THERE I WAS LETTING THEM SPEAK AND UNLOAD
THEIR BURDENS, THEIR CARES, AND THEIR WEIGHTS ON ME
TO GIVE THEM RELIEF.

I WAS GIVING THEM THE GIFT OF NOT JUDGING THEM,
NOT TALKING ABOUT THEM... NOT ARGUING WITH THEM
AND I COULD TELL BY THEIR STARE THAT THEY KNEW THAT I CARED
AND HOW PRECIOUS WOULD BE MY GIFT.

I THOUGHT I HAD NOTHING TO GIVE.
AND SO I SAID TO MYSELF,
"I WILL GIVE FORGIVENESS AWAY AS A GIFT."

I WILL FORGIVE THEM FOR EVERYTHING THEY EVER DID TO ME,
AND EVERYTHING THEY EVER SAID ABOUT ME-
ALL THE PAIN AND THE AGONY THEY CAUSED ME.

AND YES, I WAS EVEN GOING TO FORGIVE THE UNFORGIVABLE.
NO MATTER HOW EXTREME THE VIOLATION,
THE PAIN, THE OFFENSE- I WAS LETTING IT GO.

AND I KNEW I COULD DO THIS!
BECAUSE WHO AM I NOT TO FORGIVE?

WHEN AS UNTHINKABLE AS IT MAY BE, IT COULD BE ME
NEEDING TO BE FORGIVEN FOR SOME VILE,
DESPICABLE CRIME AGAINST SOMEONE.

AND IF THAT SOMEONE WERE TO GIVE ME
THE GIFT THAT I COULD NEVER BUY?
HOW PRECIOUS WOULD BE MY GIFT.

I THOUGHT I HAD NOTHING TO GIVE.
AND SO, I SAID TO MYSELF,
"I WILL GIVE MY LOVE AWAY AS A GIFT."

I WOULD GIVE MY LOVE TO SOMEONE WHO WAS UNDESERVING OF IT-
SOMEONE WHO WOULD HAVE THE NERVE TO ASK FOR IT,
THEN ABUSE IT, NEGLECT IT, ABANDON IT,
AND THEN COME BACK AND ASK FOR IT AGAIN,

SAYING THINGS WERE GOING TO CHANGE,
KNOWING IT WOULD STILL BE THE SAME.

BUT DIDN'T I SAY I WAS GOING TO GIVE MY LOVE AWAY AS A GIFT?

MY LOVE- IRREVERSIBLE, NON-NEGOTIABLE LOVE
LOVE MISTREATED, LOVE ABANDONED, AND LOVE BETRAYED,
BUT NOT SWAYED BY THAT!

BECAUSE THE LOVE THAT I WAS GOING TO GIVE,
I KNEW IN MY HEART I WOULD NEVER TAKE IT BACK.
AND HOW PRECIOUS WOULD BE MY GIFT.

WORDS MATTER

What's in a word?
Who better to answer that question than the tongue?
In fact, if anyone wishes to speak to the essence of a man,
Then by all means talk to his tongue.
It's amazing how much information can be obtained
From a simple conversation.
Even in the midst of lies,
The heart of a man is revealed through his words.
The true answers to questions like-
Who are you, where did you come from, and where are you going
Are hidden behind the words.
They are revealed in tone, quality of speech,
And the knowledge behind words.
It's been said that the heart knows many secrets,
But the tongue will tell them all.
The tongue, though small in size
Has been endowed with the power to create or destroy.
One only has to look around
To see the power of words spoken by someone.
In essence, words are invisible matter
Birthed from the womb of the mouth
With a purpose to become whatever we say.

#WordsMatter #Worddown #Wordup

YES

I PRAY THAT MY LIFE WILL BECOME A YES,
WHILE TRAVELING THROUGH UNCHARTED COURSES
OF TUMULTUOUS TERRAIN— NO REFRAIN.

YES—
THROUGH AVALANCHES OF NOES
OCEANS OF I CAN'TS
RIVERS OF MAYBES
AND MOUNTAINS OF IMPOSSIBILITIES!

A YES THAT IMPRISONS ME
AND A **YES** THAT SETS ME FREE

They're TELLIN It!

They stretch the globe far and wide,
Telling the truth, mixed in with lies.
Their faces will never give them away,
But the tongue of the gossiper is sure to betray.

The confidence of a friend, so dear
Who pours out their heart to an open ear.
In a moment of pain, anger, and stress
You tell them your secrets and all of your mess.

They listen intently from beginning to end,
Watching each gesture and taking it in.
It's amazing how sincere they appear to be,
When they vow not to tell, repeatedly.

"You have my word," at least that's what they say.
So, you sigh in relief– but then comes the day!
When the secrets you've told are released to the press,
And the little you've shared is an even bigger mess.

'Cause some things that they told, you know you did not say,
But they added some more to give it the flavor of exaggeration
And now it's real bad!
So, you try to save face 'cause you know you've been had.

And the only thing left for you to do
Is to prepare for the next time this happens to you.
So take out a pen and jot down this note,
And carry it around with you like a bag or a tote.

The gossiper can be a friend or a foe
Who can't keep a secret; they tell all that they know!
So don't look at appearances; that's not a good clue.
Just listen to everything; their lips will tell you.

Now, put yourself in the place of that soul
Who told them their business and think just how cold
The heart of this person really must be.
And if they did it to them, they'll do it to me!

He Loves You

Can you understand the vastness?
Can you comprehend the depth of His love for you?

Then, why are voices in your head
Reminding you and rewinding you back
To a moment, a mistake, a relationship
In the past that you regret, but can't forget?
How many times must He forgive you again
For the same sin?
He sees you.
In the distance, and He cries out to you!
He even tries to keep you from listening to the love that lies.
He longs to spend time with you–
The Creator longs to spend time with the creation.
Imagine that He delights in you–
The worst you
The impossible you
The you that won't even let Him in!
To think that with His power
He could erase you, yet He chooses to embrace you.
And you keep trying to earn love that is free.

Can you understand the vastness?
Can you comprehend the depth of His love for you?

WANTED

UNFORGIVENESS
ARMED AND DANGEROUS
RESPONSIBLE FOR CRIMES OF PASSION
NOTORIOUS FOR DIVIDING FAMILIES
AND DESTROYING RELATIONSHIPS
A CANCER TO THE HUMAN SOUL
MANKIND, BEWARE!

NO MATTER HOW PAINFUL
A WRONG THAT WAS DONE TO SOMEONE,
UNFORGIVENESS WILL ULTIMATELY
BECOME THEIR GREATER ENEMY.

YOU SEE, IT'S WHEN A PERSON CHOOSES
TO FORGIVE THAT THEY GAIN THE POWER
TO LET GO AND MOVE ON

IT GIVES THEM THE STRENGTH TO LEAVE THOSE
UNPLEASANT MEMORIES IN THE PAST—
SOON TO BE FORGOTTEN.

WHEN THEY CHOOSE NOT TO FORGIVE
IT JUSTIFIES THEIR ANGER
AND THEIR NEED TO AVENGE THEIR PAIN.

OVER AND OVER, IN THE COURT OF THEIR MINDS
ACTING AS THEIR ATTORNEY,
UNFORGIVENESS PRESENTS THE FACTS.

"HERE IS THE EVIDENCE:
THIS IS WHAT HAPPENED TO YOU."

THEN, THE PAST GETS PLAYED REPEATEDLY,
'TILL ANGER AND RAGE IGNITE WITHIN THEM.
THEN ONE DAY, THEY'LL WAKE UP AND REALIZE

THAT WHILE THEY WERE BEING
STALKED BY THEIR HATRED AND THEIR
NEED TO AVENGE THEIR PAIN

THEY BECAME BLINDED
TO THE BEAUTY OF EACH PASSING DAY.

AND WHILE THEIR VENGEFUL HEART WAS
CARRYING THE PAIN OF YESTERDAY,
UNFORGIVENESS WAS ROBBING THEM
OF THE JOYS OF TOMORROW.

Expose on Lies

From the time that it's uttered
'Til its final demise,
Who knows the destruction
That is caused by a lie?

For a simple untruth
Finds its way to an ear
To someone who'll listen,
To someone who'll hear.

Now, a lie has no conscience,
No guilt or remorse.
To cover the truth,
Is the plight of its course.

A lie uses people
For its own selfish needs,
As a means to destroy them.
If you lie – listen, please!

If you tell but one lie,
And just watch the effects.
A little lie gets bigger
To the liar's regret.

And the difficult task,
An impossibility,
Is to babysit a lie
In its originality.

So, you memorize the lie,
And you rehearse it in your head.
But the passing of time
Makes you forget the lie you said.

So, the tiniest lie
Has a snowball effect
To continue to grow
To the liar's regret.

Lies tell more lies;
That's all that they do.
A lie will even lie
And swear to tell the truth.

Because your lie never
Intended to be your way out.
It was a temporary fix,
But you will be found out.

And one day the truth
Will show up at your door
And your lies will not have
Your back anymore.

A GOD CONVERSATION

In a world of debates, debating.
What is the truth about God?
Humanity sighs, sighing.

Because they are frustrated
By their frustrations, frustrating them.
They keep trying to figure out answers
Without having asked the right questions.

They have become consumed with their own seekings,
But never findings, their own searchings, but never
Discovering, and their own philosophies, philosophizing
Them into believing truths from unknown sources.

Mankind has got to dig deeper to find the truth.
If God is God, can't He speak for Himself?

Would the Creator have a problem introducing Himself
To any of us, if we would just ask?

I ask these questions, questioning the
Unfathomable mysteries of His existence.

I ask, asking to know, knowing that the
Answers are for those who genuinely seek,
Seeking unknown ventures into a deep place.

It is for those who are willing to go beyond
What they can see, seeing that His physicality
Is not really physical. He is Spirit- love, loving
A world so much that He'd send His only Son

To die, dying for a world that would reject,
Rejecting the truth that Jesus died
Was buried, and would rise, rising from the
Grave to give eternal life

To as many who would believe,
Believing (John 3:16) and not forgetting
To consider (John 3:17), for He did not send
Him into the world to condemn, condemning us
For mistakes that He already knew we would make.

But it was through His death that we could be
Forgiven, forgiving us forever, when we ask
And this is the Gospel!

And this is the evidence that He is God,
Our God who provides the very air that we
Breathe, breathing air that He provides for us
Everyday. We have to depend, depending on Him

For everything we need, needing Him for food,
Water, shelter, and protection. And this is just
The beginning of a list, listing requests, requesting
Solutions to problems that are endless.

And we continue to pray, praying to a God that
We don't even know who, in spite of us–
Our mistakes, our failures, and our sins–
Loves Loving us.

He even understands, Understanding
Our human reasoning and how difficult it is
For us to believe, believing the possibility of
His existence.

Therefore, He is open to having
A God conversation with us to prove, proving
How real He is. Therefore we have His permission
To ask Him to introduce Himself to us.

Something He is all too willing to do
And the moment we ask Him to come
Into our hearts and to forgive, forgiving us for our
Unspeakable sins.

That is the prayer He is waiting to hear that links,
Linking us to eternity with Him, forever

Amen!

CRUCICIDAL.

I'm crucicidal.
I'm lost without You.
I'm not too proud to say,
"Lord, I need You."

Lord, here I am.
Where you lead me, I will go.

Father, there's a cry
That's coming from my heart
And it's louder than any other cry.
It is the prayer of all my prayers
The longing of my soul is for
You, Lord, more of You

Sometimes, I feel like the
Prodigal son, on the run
In church, I'm praising You
My hands are raised up to You,
But my heart is far from You.

In a place, I'm standing on the
Outside looking in.

I'm crucicidal.
I'm lost without You.
I'm not too proud to say,
"Lord, I need You."

Lord, here I am
Where You lead me, I will go.

Lord, I need to be consumed by You
In Your presence, seeking You
Loving You, obeying You.

I need Lord, to overdose on You
To be hacked out of my mind
And become crucicidal for You.

Father, there's a cry
That's coming from my heart
And it's louder than any other cry.
It is the prayer of all my prayers
The longing of my soul is for You,
Lord, more of You.

The WHO-NEVERS

We won't be there
At the many family gatherings
Held throughout the years.
You'll never see our faces.
And if there's any consolation for us,
This message represents our tears.

    Our early departure was your sigh of relief,
      When you did what you felt you had to do.
    We were anxiously waiting for life to show up.
And to our disappointment, it never came through.

If only our voices
Could've been heard from the womb
As we listened to the plans
For our quick demise.

NOOOOOOO!

WE WANT TO LIVE!
WE WANT TO LIVE!

PLEASE DON,T KILL US!
WE,RE TOO YOUNG TO DIE!

Now we know that they told you
That we were a bunch of cells,
And not yet human.
But how could that be?

They lied,
Because the same amount of time in the womb
That it took to give birth to a "You"
Is what we needed to give birth to a "Me."

Imagine the envy we had towards those who
Successfully made it through the birth canal of life.
Life for us was over before it started.
We never saw the day, only a long dark night.

So we're the "Who's" that were left undone.
And we missed our God-given opportunity
To become anyone.

We never laughed; we never cried.
In fact, the entire account of our existence
Is that we lived and were forced to die.

We never felt our mother's touch.
And our father's gaze
Would've meant so much.

                                No brother's bond
                                No sister's care
                                And if we were loved,
                                We were not aware

WE NEVER GOT A CHANCE TO RUN AND PLAY.
<u>NO</u> WORDS EXPRESS OUR BIRTH!
<u>NO</u> DATES!
<u>NO</u> DAYS.

This is a message that represents our tears.
In the womb, we alone, felt the terror.
And we wish you could've felt our fears.

                    We are the "Who's" who never will weep.
                    We'll never shout, but our blood flows deep.

Mom... Dad...
We're not trying to condemn you
For an atrocity that was done
Perhaps in the midst of your fears.

                    But in spite of the way that things turned out,
                                We're still your children,
                    And this message represents our tears.

We forgive you.
And if you dwell in the valley of regret,
You have yourself to forgive.
We're dwelling in our heavenly home now,
And this is a beautiful place to live.

Approximately 1.5 billion babies
Were sucked, torn, and ripped
Unmercifully from the womb.

The next time you see, touch, or embrace a child,
Understand that "NO CHOICE"
Could've happened to them.
And if we're completely honest,
It could've happened to you.

We're asking you to respond to the cries of the unborn,
Who are about to expire and they don't know why.
Listen intently as they cry out,

**"WE WANT TO LIVE!
WE WANT TO LIVE!
PLEASE DON'T KILL US,
WE'RE TOO YOUNG TO DIE."**

About the Author

Karen Brown is a writer and spoken word artist who ventures into poetic personifications that express the cries of the human soul. She has written and performed works on grief, addiction, mistakes, and much more. Her words challenge the listener and reader to face underlying soul entanglements. Her vision is to arouse discussions that take her audience to a place called truth. She wants to encourage them through her lyrical persuasions to confront their guilt, admit their mistakes, and abandon unforgivable offenses that come to rob us all.

Throughout her life, she learned that humility and not pride will keep you from thinking more highly of yourself than you ought, that forgiveness has a power that few people will ever discover, and that sorrow is a lonely path. But most importantly, she learned that there is a Comforter beyond this world! She learned that when she didn't understand things that happened in her life, she could ask the Creator questions, and in His own way, He would find a way to answer her.

Karen loves and enjoys her family that is rich in love, laughter, talent, and the ability to enjoy each other's company. Throughout her life, she has managed to set aside time to go visit and care for some special people that she met along the way, and they have become her extended family. She is the founder of an organization that delivers an #iPrayForPeople message to all who'll listen.